Secrets of a broken heart

Corrine Parkins

BookLeaf Publishing

Presentation by *BookLeaf Publishing*

Web: www.bookleafpub.com

E-mail: info@bookleafpub.com

ISBN : 9789357699587

First edition 2022

DEDICATION

My breasties April and Sabrina; Auriel-you are more like a sister to me than just a friend. My family-blood or not, my friends-my tribe you all know who you are, and I owe you so much for all that you have done to support me and my kids through some of the most heartbreaking events of our lives. For being there, even at my worst when I didn't feel like I deserved your friendship. Lastly, Amanda for being my guide on my journey to healing; I would not be where I am today without you.

ACKNOWLEDGEMENT

Whether it is loss of a relationship, loved one, or even loss of ones sense of self. It's during my depression that I came across some poetry by Nikita Gill that resonated with me. Her words were so exquisite and quite literally spoke to how I felt; it inspired me to start writing my own poems as a part of my healing process.

PREFACE

A breath of fresh air, finally able to exhale. A glimpse into my mind of all that lingers there... as I bloom into who I am meant to be. This is my breakthrough; standing up, screaming out and declaring that I have a voice.

Poem 1

Sticks and stones may break my bones, but your words bruise and scar me. I obsess in my mind, overthinking and doubting the things that you say. Confused of why you would say such horrendous things to me, that are now seared into my brain, never to forget and yet things I could never bring myself to say out loud. You used to call me baby and say sweet things... don't call me by my name, that's how I know something is wrong. It cuts so deep, chastising me like I was in trouble, making me feel shame.

Jigsaw puzzle

Memories are just bits and pieces, like a messed up jigsaw puzzle, I'm trying to fit the pieces together and I don't know how. Some I don't want to fit, but they do and it's a part of who I am. Forgetting, or trying to convince myself that I don't want or need to feel those memories causes more questions, pain, and doubt in who I am because I don't know what to do with all of these pieces and how they fit into my puzzle quite yet.

Broken home

A house is not a home when you burn it down. Like flames my screams shatter the glass; there are no memories worth keeping. Arson...the pain I feel is my arsenal and I will throw it back at you. You don't get to set me on fire and play the victim this time, I will burn you and you will never touch me or have a memory of who you want me to be ever again. When home is broken, burned, and taken from me you don't get to tell me how to feel. Home is supposed to be a safe place and you took that from me. So, home isn't where the heart is, it's where my broken heart is, where memories are forgotten and have turned to painful triggers of what wasn't real, but what was fake....it haunts me. I shared my deepest and darkest secrets and fears with you, seeking safety... and you took them and played them back to me like a nightmare, making them a horrifying reality.

Depression

Happiness is a daily fight, if you're like me. They say choose your battles wisely, but this one chooses you. You take a daily pill, it's almost like candy in hopes that it will magically change how you feel. People say to "get over it", "it's all in your head", or "it could be worse"; but that belittles me and dismisses my feelings. We don't get over it, we get through it.

Beauty is Pain

The pain we endure to attain beauty... but what is beauty in the eye of the beholder? Society ingrains standards of beauty and what it is, what it looks like. Breaking those boundaries, shattering the standards all come at a price. Finding those pieces of self love, acceptance, and the true worth compete with insecurities that literally eat away our hearts, bodies, and our souls-who we are to the core. Questions of "will you still love me if?" "what is my worth/value to you?" "Am I good enough or when will I be good enough?" If only I could see myself the way that others do, but that's a fear too. What do people see when they look at me? They can't possibly see the pain I feel, they don't know my thoughts and how I mentally tear myself apart and want to cut away the parts I find to be ugly flaws in hopes that it will make me feel or look better. How can someone so fragile be so strong and yet break so easily?

The beauty in the dark

There is beauty in darkness and darkness in beauty. Those two ideas are separate with their own meaning, they are not interchangeable concepts. In the darkness there is mystery to the unknown, something to be discovered, and to the right person can be exquisite; to the wrong person it can be misunderstood and unappreciated. It is through beauty that people are blinded from someone's darkness. We don't see what's lurking in the shadows of what's hidden: pain, trauma, insecurities, and millions of other things that we hide from others because maybe we're afraid to share those raw truths about ourselves. It is the darkness that can be cold and horrifying, but it can also be peaceful-peace in the silence. What lurks in the darkness are the things we bury deep; monsters... fears.

Poem 7

I just want to sleep, and drown in the darkness. I didn't think that my home and what was safe could be taken from me again... and yet it was. I'm expendable, just throw me aside and find someone else to get what you want and need-because it's not me. I can't be what you want, or what you need; maybe I never was and never could be. Unwanted, unloved, used... You shut me out and kept hidden from me and secrets. Don't say you're sorry, do you even know what to be sorry for? Are you sorry for using me, because I was naive? Or are you sorry I found out?

Poem 8

Drink to numb the pain and bury it deep. It creeps up my throat like vomit that burns when you try and swallow the tears. I try to forget... I scream quietly in my mind and want to cry, to hide in the darkness and let the tears roll; muffle my sobs so no one can hear me.

Beast

Fear me, like I fear myself. Don't look at me, because I don't look at myself. I've been told you can't love anyone else if you don't love yourself. I don't believe that... I love others more than I love myself. In reality... isn't love just a lie that you tell to someone's face?

Screams

The screaming in my head is so loud, it's deafening, but when I open my mouth I'm mute. Don't feel...I don't want to feel these ugly things because they're so painful. Be quiet, don't speak... he likes me better that way-I talk too much. Keep it in, keep it to myself, bottle it and bury it deep. Don't feel, it makes me sick and makes me want to vomit and cry.

Shatters

Damaged goods or damaged heart? That is me-damaged and broken, will I ever be whole again? I compete with myself and everyone else. My heart is shattered, it can't be fixed when I keep cutting and stabbing myself with shards of pain... memories that run deep. Why me? When I poison myself and my thoughts. Can I be a choice? I want to be the one, but I get lost in the crowd-you won't find me. No on sees me, I'm invisible and that's why I get passed by. I'm nothing and no one, I'm a barrier, a door mat to stomp on; you threw me away like a piece of trash-indispensable like I meant nothing to you. They're not here to see me, they look right through me because they know they're better. Free my mind from the prison of my thoughts; I wish I could blow the thoughts out of my mind, to rip my heart out and not feel anymore because the pain is absolute torture.

Blindness

Out of sight, out of mind... but the things said are in my mind. How do I not take them personally? I can't see them, but I hear them and feel them. Thoughts that circle around my brain, festering like a disease... eating, rotting away at me; questioning me, doubting. It's also the silence of what's not said; the fear of the truth and meanings of the unspoken. What's worse? Not knowing and anticipating with fear, or knowing and the heartbreak and pain that go along with it? That pain is agonizing... you would rather die than let them see you cry.

Bloom

My tears used to fall, like petals from a flower; my soul slowly dying with the aching pain of my broken heart, longing for you. I'm slowly piecing my heart back together, the pain in my chest becoming less and less. I'm starting to bloom.

Silence in heartbreak

When a heart breaks does anybody hear it? Does anybody feel it? Only the one silently breaking and shattering to the floor. It's like an internal bleed that suffocates the life out of you. As you stand there... helpless, bleeding your heart out and yet there's no one that can save you.

Sleep with your eyes closed

If I wake in the middle of the night, will you be there? What if I wake up multiple times because I can't sleep, from my deep anxiety? Will you be there, or hidden away in the shadows like a secret? When I wake in the morning will you be there? Or will you hide then too, because you're afraid of the light? I don't need or want someone to be my night, I have enough darkness on my own. I need and want someone to be my light.

Scars

Words can break you, cut you like glass- they eat away at you like acid melting your heart. Words can mean everything from the wrong person, and also mean nothing from the one who matters the most. Words are like death, when you make them sweet lies left for me to choke on. It's those lies that have no meaning when you breath them, and yet they're intoxicating and I'm desperate for their taste, their truth. Why do you suffocate me, drown me with your lies? Better yet, why do I swallow them like it doesn't hurt?

Tragedy

You murdered us... like a tragic love story. I wanted you... but you didn't want me; throw away the broken pieces of me. Would you like me more if I was like her? I can try and be more like her... But you'd always tell me you loved me for the way I am, and never to change. Did you really love me for... me, or did you love how naive I was? Like Romeo & Juliet our love was forbidden; they tell me to pretend you're dead, but how can I when you are standing right in front of me? I can't hate you, even if I tried. You lied, and I cried an ocean of tears that almost suffocated and drowned me... and all that grew was a divide in our love, forever lost and forever broken.

Spill

I was your sun- I gave you light and thought I could heal you. You were my moon, but you brought me darkness and were cold. How can something so comforting and trusting be so damaging at the same time? The light gave me life, and yet the darkness was yours. I poured myself into you to fill you up, but I spilled over the edges. You drank me up and swallowed me whole, just to spit me out.

Loving memories

I reminisce the memories I have of you... and us, and it's bittersweet. The truth hurts, it was absolutely painful. I learned lessons the hard way... but oh did I learn. I don't regret the time we spent together, I cherish the good times we had. I keep a piece of you forever in my soul; although you broke my heart a piece of it will always be yours. My heart is finally on the mend, and although we can never be together, deep down inside a small part of me will always care for you and hope you find the healing you need.

Awaken

With arms outstretched, I welcome the sun and the warmth it gives my soul. I open my eyes to the vivid blue sky; I inhale the crisp cold air and the faint smell of spring flowers soon to bloom. I hear the singing of the birds in the morning and I feel peace.

Queen

I am the queen of my castle, I've built my walls high for my safety... and yours. Don't think that you can tear them down that easily. Prove to me that you are worth my time and energy, that you won't hurt me, and if you're willing... climb those walls I've crafted so intricately to protect my heart. If you so much as betray my trust in any way, don't think that my storm won't rage... I will throw you out of my tower and out of my life so quickly. I don't need anyone to paint me a fake fairy tail, my dreams will come true with or without you. I told you, I am the queen, this is my castle and I answer to no one!